Inhale Comfort, Exhale Hope!

10 Funeral Homilies

Mark Randall Powell

CSS Publishing Company, Inc.
Lima, Ohio

INHALE COMFORT, EXHALE HOPE!

FIRST EDITION
Copyright © 2015
by CSS Publishing Co., Inc.

The original purchaser may print and photocopy material in this publication for use as it was intended (worship material for worship use; educational material for classroom use; dramatic material for staging or production). No additional permission is required from the publisher for such copying by the original purchaser only. Inquiries should be addressed to: Permissions, CSS Publishing Company, Inc., 5450 N. Dixie Highway, Lima, Ohio 45807.

Scripture quotations are from the New Revised Standard Version of the Bible. Copyright 1989 by the Division of Christian Education of the National Council of the Churches of Christ in the USA, Nashville, Thomas Nelson Publishers © 1989. Used by permission. All rights reserved.

Library of Congress Cataloging-in-Publication Data

Powell, Mark Randall.
 [Sermons. Selections]
 Inhale comfort, exhale hope! : 10 funeral homilies / Mark Randall Powell. -- FIRST EDITION.
    pages cm
  ISBN 0-7880-2807-3 (alk. paper)
 1. Funeral sermons. 2. Bible--Sermons. I. Title.

BV4275.P69   2014
252'.1--dc23

2014024222

For more information about CSS Publishing Company resources, visit our website at www.csspub.com, email us at csr@csspub.com, or call (800) 241-4056.

e-book:
ISBN-13: 978-0-7880-2808-3
ISBN-10: 0-7880-2808-1

ISBN-13: 978-0-7880-2807-6
ISBN-10: 0-7880-2807-3   PRINTED IN USA

Table of Contents

Introduction
The Christian Funeral and the Christian Clergy 5

A Funeral Homily From John 14
Concerning an Unexpected Death 7

A Funeral Homily From Psalm 116
Concerning the Death of an Elderly Christian 13

A Funeral Homily From 1 Corinthians 15
Concerning the Death of Death 19

A Funeral Homily From 1 Thessalonians 4:13-18
Concerning the Joyful Promise of Future Resurrection ... 25

A Funeral Homily From 2 Corinthians 1
Concerning the God of Mercy and Consolation 31

A Funeral Homily From Isaiah 40:27-31
Concerning the Death of Someone Unknown to the Pastor . 37

A Funeral Homily From John 13
Concerning a Death from Suicide 43

A Funeral Homily From Psalm 13
Concerning the Death of a Child 49

A Funeral Homily From Psalm 46
Concerning the God of Refuge and Strength 57

A Funeral Homily From Hebrews 4
Concerning the Death of a Young Person by Accident.... 61

Introduction

The Christian Funeral and the Christian Clergy

With the end of Christendom and the rise of hyper-modernism, members of the wider community no longer find even an inner-need for the teachings or the practices of organized religion. The general community may be having a conversation about spiritual ideas, but if they are, the church's presence is no longer required.

This is simply true.

That is, it is true with the exception of the Christian funeral, which remains the one opportunity for a pastor to touch the hearts of the expanded community setting, beyond the congregation. In facing the death of a friend or loved one those gathered for the funeral will usually, perhaps out of respect for the occasion, offer the clergy an opportunity to officiate and to share their thoughts on what this drama of life and death really means. It seems that death still brings forward a more attentive gathering.

The clergy must be very watchful over this opportunity. I understand why some would disagree, but I would contend that this hour is expressly not the moment for evangelism, but instead this is the setting for truth. To say this differently, the funeral experience must take on the reality of the moment and not a canned message. The clergy presider must be part of the suffering community — legitimate in her own grief and in her own knowledge of the brokenness of the human condition. Anything less is to pretend, and believe me, pretense is the death of the homiletic moment.

Another word for what I am describing is authenticity.

All clergy must find their own way here. But after some time and with the experience of many ministry moments, we begin to develop our own way of meeting the demands of authenticity. A sort of ministry seasoning occurs, and this seasoning gives the pastor an innate credibility before the funeral gathering, a credibility that must be present if the listeners are to offer their attention past the first thirty seconds of the homily.

These funeral homilies comprise the seasoning that has developed in my nearly forty years of ministry. They are offered not as *the* way of the funeral homily, but rather as *a* way. As such, I hope they encourage other pastors to think about the themes of the funeral homily through my lens for a while, but only as a path toward a refreshment of their own.

Having said this, you will notice no attempt has been made to be innovative and neither have I flinched from redundancy. As I have said, I believe there are basic themes to the funeral homily — the world is a mess, we live and we die, but there is hope because God is present — and these themes must be sounded again and again.

In fact, I would argue that the funeral demands repetition. Think about it. Here we stand before a family grieving out their guts, how do we expect them to hear or let alone remember what we say in a funeral homily? They simply cannot do so. But they can be reminded of what they have heard time and time again at funeral after funeral. For me, to strike faith's muscle-memory is my pastoral purpose on that day.

This is why a few days afterward I often share a copy of my funeral homily with the grieving family. This offers them an opportunity to reflect and think through the gift of the Lord — the gift that is his word and his words of life.

It is my same hope for these ten homilies. I hope they allow a reflection on the gift that is the Lord of life, and that they become an encouragement to both clergy and parishioners alike, as we walk this long road of grief.

Mark Randall Powell

A Funeral Homily From John 14

Concerning an Unexpected Death

I have chosen to base this homily upon a crucial text from Saint John's gospel, the fourteenth chapter. Many Bible scholars describe today's reading as part of an extended passage known as Jesus' "farewell discourse." These scholars understand Jesus to be sharing words of assurance with his friends because he knew they would soon face the world without his earthly presence. And, in fact, we find in today's reading a most intimate conversation between Jesus and his disciples prior to the calamity of his state execution. Clearly, Jesus intends these words to inhale comfort and exhale hope!

For our purposes today, which after all are quite serious, I have decided to allow this text to bring into focus just three of Jesus' statements of consolation, finding in his ancient words of encouragement a much needed comfort for ourselves as well.

First, Jesus promises: "I will not leave you orphaned" (v. 18).

What a captivating promise for both the disciples and for us. You see, with the reality of his impending death racing toward them, and knowing how this would occur through the brutality of crucifixion, Jesus understands that one possible conclusion from his followers would be that his words and works would become futile. That is, these believers might easily surmise from his execution that his words and his works died with him. What good is a dead prophet, after all?

Or, said differently, with the plunging weight of grief from Jesus' death it might be natural for his followers to conclude that they had been orphaned! But Jesus refutes this fear outright, asserting that nothing could be further from the truth.

An orphan stands devoid of guidance or guardian, but Jesus promises that he has no intention of leaving them, not even in death! In fact, he says this exactly: "In a little while the world will no longer see me, but you will see me; because I live, you also will live" (v. 19).

How these believers needed to hear these words! But brothers and sisters, how we need to hear them as well. Let us be thankful that the promise of God as guard and guide is no less true for us than it was for those original followers. To be sure, none of us knew what we would face this [Monday] past, but God — who did not cause this death — knew exactly what was happening, and as our guardian and guide he was the first to cry, and even now he weeps with us.

This is true! Believe it!

We are not orphaned. God was present as the doctor spoke the pronouncement; God was present when this shattering sadness split open our hearts; God was present as we came to face the reality of this funeral day. And God will be present as we continue on this dark road of grief.

Take note that Jesus describes this strength that sustains us as coming from the Comforter, the one ever-present to us and the one ever-standing beside us. The text actually names this Comforter, calling him the Holy Spirit, and as the Holy Spirit of God's presence the Comforter stands as close to us as the air we breathe.

Do we need the comfort of the Lord? If we will but engage the almighty in the prayer moment, if we will but face with honesty our grief — focusing our minds on the Comforter's surrounding presence — then suddenly we find we are not orphaned at all. Suddenly, we find ourselves lifted and carried along by our ever-present guardian and guide.

Second, Jesus says to his followers,

> But the advocate, the Holy Spirit, whom the Father will send in my name, will teach you everything, and remind you of all that I have said to you. Peace I leave with you; my peace I give to you. I do not give to you as the world gives. Do not let your hearts be troubled, and do not let them be afraid.
> (vv. 26-27)

In this portion of the conversation Jesus offers such a subtle word of comfort that, if not heard carefully, it may go unnoticed. Here Jesus declares that after his departure there will be no need for believers to remember his promises because the Comforter will remind them of his every caring word.

This promise would affirm Jesus' presence to his disciples, but these same words of encouragement come rushing forward toward us as well. As we attempt to see through the gloom of this present chaos it might be easy to forget the many and varied comforting words from the Lord. Or it may be in the months of mourning that lie ahead — when something reminds you of your husband, or Pop, or friend — you might despair over the durability of God's love for you, fearing that his love will fail and that you will be overwhelmed.

Do not worry. The text promises us that the words of the Lord will be present to us right when we need to hear them. In fact, the Spirit's ongoing task will be to strengthen us during our suffering, urging us toward hope by reminding us of the Savior's care.

But there is more. Notice the type of comfort offered. The text proclaims that Jesus offers "peace of mind and heart."

Peace of mind and heart. In our present circumstances how we need this promise to be real, especially when we consider how suddenly our loved one died, leaving only the fractures found in "what-ifs" and "how-comes." Truly, these grief-questions bring troubled hearts and brooding minds, but when we turn toward Jesus' words we see that as the chaos grows darker and darker the clear light of God's peace — a true peace that passes human understanding — shines even brighter into the heart of sorrow.

The world offers a momentary peace based upon things and circumstances. But what happens when our things rust and our circumstances turn dire, as they have now? What happens when we feel the heavy breath of death's voice in our ear? What then? It is then that the still, small voice of the Comforter whispers to us. It is then that the subtle promise of Jesus to his followers takes a powerful turn toward us. Peace of mind and heart? Yes, Lord, we'll take that! We need it desperately.

But listen closely. You who have genuinely offered yourselves to the living, risen Christ, you already reside in the midst of that peace! You may not feel the blessed peace that passes understanding carrying you, steadying you, but you need only ask just where your heart and mind would be if not for the present power of the Spirit resting on you.

So my brothers and sisters, I counsel you, I urge you: rest surely in this whispered peace, walk in it by faith, for it is the Lord's everlasting arms that hold you, and his great gift of daily assurance that sustains you.

Finally, Jesus says,

> Do not let your hearts be troubled. Believe in God, believe also in me. In my Father's house there are many dwelling places. If it were not so, would I have told you that I go to prepare a place for you? And if I go and prepare a place for you, I will come again

and will take you to myself, so that where I am, there you may be also.
(vv. 1-3)

In Jesus' mind the darkness of his hour called for frankness. He levels with his followers — I'm leaving; I am about to die. This is the way of all flesh. We all have an appointment with someone like the owner of this funeral home, but notice how Jesus stoutly pushes against the finality of this death appointment. Here he gives to his followers, and by extension to us, his most precious promise: "I have a place for you...."

In essence Jesus is saying, "Yes, I will die, but that does not end the story, and one day you will be with me and we will again hang out like this, forever."

What a precious word of comfort.

I share this so that you will set before your minds the important reminder that a future stands strongly beyond hospital beds and graveyards! I share this so you know that while death may be the way of all flesh, death does not have the final word! We know that those who have offered allegiance to the living, risen Christ possess at the very heart of their being this powerful promise, this blessed hope of life eternal. In today's reading notice how the assurance of hope comes from the lips of Jesus himself. And it is here we find his most comforting promise of all: "If this were not true, I would have told you...." Hear it again: "If this were not true, I would have told you...."

Let me remind you that while our [Brother] is not here, it doesn't follow that he is nowhere. On the authority of the living word of God we would declare to you that he is in that placed promised and prepared by the Lord for his people, and so shall he ever be with the Lord.

We will never get over the events of this week; we are not supposed to. But we will get through these events. We will survive. We will endure because of the reality of God's continued presence and because of the Spirit's moment-by-moment whispers of promise, his subtle reminders of hope that tell us that this place of death where we now stand is not the final place.

A Funeral Homily From Psalm 116

Concerning the Death of an Elderly Christian

Brothers and sisters: A member of the family has died which means we finally must face that day we knew would arrive. We are never really prepared for such a day as this because we are never really ready to say good-bye to our loved ones. But today forces us to acknowledge reality; we must admit the loss of our loved one and our friend. She no longer inhabits her accustomed place beside us. Now we must discover a new life-balance and in some way we must redefine our lives without her counsel and without her love.

On this day grief truly holds onto our hearts, but I must confess that as I prepared for this homily I also found a strange sense of joy welling up within. I wonder if you too can recognize some sense of joy within your heart as well?

How so?

We certainly can admit to joy because she no longer suffers such a grave and debilitating affliction. And perhaps we can admit to joy because she now, somehow, entwines her life with those loved ones who waited so long for her arrival. Or finally, we may even be able to admit to joy because she now dwells with the Lord whom she loved and who secured her heart so many, many years ago. Think about this day in this way: Our sister in Christ now lives in freedom! Let us find in ourselves a way to be glad for her even as we grieve.

As with most circumstances within the human condition, today we face a mixed-bag of emotions — grief and joy, loss and hope. Therefore, in order to discover a path upon which to start our walk of grief and to maintain the hopeful heart we know she would wish for us, I have decided to base today's funeral homily upon what has become for me a most cherished text from the Hebrew Bible.

Today we will hear a scripture that offers a simple but compelling reminder of the almighty's loving presence in the lives of his people, and today we will hear from scripture a reassuring testimony that speaks a subtle but potent assurance of the reality of God's hope-filled promises in the lives of his people. God's presence and God's promises inhabit today's task.

To this end I ask that you now attend your minds to a reading of the living word of God. The Hebrew poet writes in Psalm 116:15: "Precious in the sight of the Lord is the death of his faithful ones."

Listen to this text again: "Precious in the sight of the Lord is the death of his faithful ones."

Immediately we are overtaken by the idea of the Lord's sight — "Precious in the sight of the Lord..." reads the text.

I am not sure we usually think of the Lord as in some way having sight, but the poet's metaphor clearly affirms this very idea. And yet, the assertion of God's sight may raise questions. If the poet speaks the truth, if God sees, then this changes the world does it not? We would abruptly realize, for example, that God does not preside over the creation as some absentee landlord, initially forwarding the motion of natural law and then leaving it to wind down as it would. On the contrary, based upon this text, if God sees then God watches. If God watches then God stands in ultimate awareness. If God stands in ultimate awareness then God cares.

If God sees then God cares — let us think about this axiom as the central reality of truth.

We could voice this central truth in this way: God does not exist as the man in the sky, benevolent but detached and devoid of responsibility. This popular caricature of God is meaningless and therefore useless. Instead, we could learn from this text that if God sees then God abides close to us in a self-chosen obligation to his world, electing to be present to the creation and to those who wish to know him. We could learn from this text that God stands fully engaged with his world, not once denying his care for this, his place, not once forgetting his desire for justice and mercy to meet and kiss. Finally, we could learn from this text that God continually moves toward his world and his people with an ongoing providential love, noting especially the passing away of those faithful and those precious to him.

This means God sees it all. God sees the savage truth of the human condition. God sees the truth we face in death, hating its brutality as it hounds and pounds his people. God sees the brokenness of the world and desires for it new life and a new way to live, and who by the sheer action of his grace accomplished that very desire through Jesus, the Christ. God sees the illnesses of his people, including that of our loved one.

This would only begin to plumb the depth of what the text means when it says God sees and therefore God cares. We could voice this central truth reality in a different way. We could say that God's most precious gift to us is life itself. This gift must never be taken for granted or squandered.

The almighty means for us to enjoy this life throughout whatever time we have, but life only truly flourishes within his enduring purpose. We find this purpose within the vocation given us by God himself, who calls us to stand beside the one in need because we genuinely love him when we love others. This means to squander life on one's own appetites and whims truly bears the label of sin — that may ultimately be defined as selfishness.

This leads us straight back to the text: "Precious in the sight of the Lord is the death of his faithful ones," which in this case means God is on the lookout for faithful ones — those who love his gift of life so thoroughly that they offer themselves in sacrificial allegiance to his ways and to his path of true humanness.

I call this manner of life "walking the Jesus way," and God watches for those who practice this outward-to-others vocation. Those who choose to walk this pathway are the faithful ones described in today's text. These are the ones who honestly love the almighty's gift of life. These are the ones the Lord finds faithful and precious to him.

These are faithful and precious to the Lord because their lives push against the selfishness of greed and hate, those actions that comprise today's all too typical way of being human. These are faithful and precious to the Lord because by faith they have taken his word and his way seriously, even though he remains unseen to them. These are faithful and precious to the Lord because they consistently walk the road of humility toward others and toward him.

Typically, the people I am describing live small lives. They impact only a few people not thousands, but God sees. Listen brothers and sisters, God sees.

No doubt God saw our loved one and our friend whose passing we mourn this day in just this way. God saw her life of giving. God saw her faithfulness in illness. God saw her body bring forth that final breath, and as she passed from us the Lord smiled in her consciousness his approval, a smile which marked her as faithful and precious.

The Lord's holy smile would have been no surprise to us, would it? We saw her loving character demonstrated all along. We discerned in her a heart for God and his ways, a love of justice and mercy and a serious affection for God's people and their mission to love the other through action.

She understood life as a gift which she accepted to mean that her life must be given away for the needy one beside her. We know this to be true because she fully shared her life with us, and by giving herself to us in love we understood we were not alone in the world. Her life gathered us closer to the Lord.

Today we mourn; today we grieve her loss because we know how much we needed her with us. She was our teacher. She inspired us to follow on, to fight the good fight, and to finish well. Few demonstrate these lessons today.

Back when Christendom flourished, back when the Christian consensus stood intact, dying well was the task of the aged Christ follower. These older, faithful ones accepted the calling to reveal to those younger believers still on the way what death in the "bosom of the Lord" actually looked like. With modern ways of dying within the blank institutional blandness of hospitals and nursing homes, much of this final teaching has been lost to us, but not altogether.

Today we stand before the memory of a woman who lived well because she lived for others. Today we mourn and celebrate a woman who before our eyes died well because she died in faithful obedience to the Lord whom she loved. And so, she teaches us still.

"Precious in the sight of the Lord is the death of his faithful ones." Yes, she is precious in the sight of the Lord, no doubt, and she is most precious in our sight as well.

A Funeral Homily From 1 Corinthians 15

Concerning the Death of Death

Today we gather and stand before the body of our brother in Christ. We come to this hour fully aware that he has left us after having lived a full life. In fact, as his pastor, I declare that our brother loved the Lord Jesus, served him faithfully, and desired others to know and serve the Lord as well. He lived his life as an honorable family man, a dependable public servant, a devoted churchman, and my good friend. All of us will miss him.

Therefore, I intend that the text I have chosen for today's home-going homily would bring some encouragement to us as we grieve for this member of our forever-family. The text comes from Saint Paul's first letter to the churches found in the city of Corinth, and it brings to us the reality of the death of death as well as the ultimate hope for new life in Christ. Both themes, as we shall see from this reading, have been formed within the sacred reality of Jesus' own resurrection.

These themes are most appropriate for today's grief work. Let us attend to a reading of the living word of God. Saint Paul writes:

Death has been swallowed up in victory.
Where, O death, is your victory?
Where, O death, is your sting?
— 1 Corinthians 15:54b-55

This is the word of the Lord!
Perhaps on the face of it we might think this a strange and even an unexpected text to choose for this hour. Likewise, we might find this a very unusual question for the great

apostle to ask. Just what does Saint Paul mean by questioning us: "Where, O death, is your sting?" Clearly, we know the answer only all too well. If you wish to know where the sting of death resides you merely need to look at the faces of this dear family sitting before me. "Where, O death, is your sting?" indeed! What a foolish question.

But before we too quickly accuse the apostle of insensitivity, let us pause for a moment and think about what his teaching could actually mean. We might find it helpful in this regard to repeat the first question Saint Paul asked in the reading. At first he demanded, "Where, O death, is your victory?" and only then does he question, "Where, O death, is your sting?"

Here we stand on solid footing; this first question makes much more sense. In fact, we could come to the meaning of the apostle's inquiry by asking the same question only from a different direction: Does death win the final victory?

That is, what if we asked ourselves the unthinkable? What if we asked what it would mean for our loved one and our friend if, in the end, death did win the complete victory? What if we asked what it would mean if death pronounced the words "gone forever" over him? What then?

Let our response be definitive and expressive: If death wins, if dead is only dead, then we have nothing more to say here, literally. A living, victorious death forces us to pack our tents and head for home, for all hope is abandoned. To be sure, we would be able to describe and celebrate the fruits of this honorable life, but if death wins the day then we are most miserable because we believe and proclaim a lie.

But thankfully, this is not the case. Thankfully, the apostle's words are presented not to mock our bereavement but instead to mock death and to announce that no such final victory shout will ever come from this hateful enemy!

Saint Paul teaches that death itself has died.

How did the great apostle come to this teaching of hope beyond the grave? He received this realization by revelation from almighty God and by his own witness to the reality of the crucified yet living, risen Jesus. This means Saint Paul proclaims to us in his letters a most trustworthy message, that the most wonderful thing has happened! Jesus is alive, truly alive, and as a result of his finished work on the cross, in the resurrection, by the ascension and through his imminent appearing, death's battlements have been thoroughly breeched and its power over us has been completely destroyed, forever!

It will be even more comforting if we dig a little deeper into the apostle's teaching by citing an earlier passage found in the same chapter as today's reading. Let us hear this text:

> But in fact Christ has been raised from the dead, the firstfruits of those who have died. For since death came through a human being, the resurrection of the dead has also come through a human being; for as all die in Adam, so all will be made alive in Christ.
> — 1 Corinthians 15:20-22

Here Saint Paul teaches that Jesus has become the "firstfruits" of resurrection. This means Jesus' resurrection will be the first of many, many more. We could say it this way: Because death could not hold the Lord, it will not hold Jesus' people either!

This truth led the great apostle to mock death in today's reading because Jesus — the living, risen Christ — shattered the power of death once and for all. Jesus, the living one, thoroughly overpowered and vanquished this great and hateful enemy as he in resolute determination willingly withstood, absorbed, and defeated the darkness of evil all the way from birth to empty tomb.

Brothers and sisters, I believe these words to be a faithful rendering of what Saint Paul means us to understand, and I believe these words represent true reality.

But, having said this, I know our questions still linger. While Saint Paul may lead us to recognize with our minds this victory over death — where O grave is your victory? — this present hour still does not feel victorious, does it? Our friend and loved one is still gone, and notwithstanding the apostle's proclamation, it does feel as though death's stinging pain has left us defeated.

"What are we to do? How do we endure this grief?"

We must admit that this present pain will continue for a time; we would be fools to pretend we do not suffer. But, brothers and sisters, we will not suffer forever! In fact, the Christian faith calls us to make a choice of faith, now, today. The truth of resurrection compels us to choose to see our grief from God's perspective. That is, resurrection — both Jesus' and our brother's — glows with authenticity, right now. And while this decision to see death from God's perspective does not mean we seek to minimize the suffering we know now, it does mean we see through this suffering as we look forward toward that day when our faith will be sight.

Naturally, we hurt now, but from the Lord's vantage point death has already been conquered by the Christ, who secured the future — through the very heart of death's dark and hateful ravages — for all those who wish to come along. This includes our brother in Christ and this includes all those who would choose to be believers in this room.

God calls us to adopt this new view of reality, today, even though darkness presently surrounds us. This calling stands at the heart of the Christian faith. This calling expressly means that while we wait for the final revealing of this new life, we presently "see through" this hour of suffering by choosing to live this moment within the sure and secure promise of this glorious resurrection reality.

Clearly, we will only be able to accomplish this seeing through our current difficulty if we keep our eyes on the living Christ, the great author and perfecter of our faith. We daily confess with our mouths and believe in our hearts that Christ is risen from the dead, and by this confession we choose to be in a living faith that accomplishes the Lord's own good work.

In fact, as we live out this faith-toward-resurrection confession we discover that it daily conforms us to the perspective of hope, a hope that cuts a very deep path through the heart of our suffering. This faith-toward-resurrection leads us beyond ourselves and our focus on loss by allowing us to become part of God's ongoing reclamation project. While we wait to participate in the final calling of resurrected redemption, our present suffering calls us to join the suffering of the world and to labor for the benefit of the Lord's good creation remade.

We do not allow our suffering to stop our discipleship, for eventually we come to realize that our faithfulness in suffering actually displays the Lord's ability to overturn the old death order right now, even as we wait for the new world to be fully realized.

Our present steadfast suffering-in-hope, therefore, is faithful discipleship at work and in reality! Our steadfast suffering-in-hope proclaims the reality of Jesus' resurrection to all who care to hear, which at its heart includes the clear and present promise of our brother in Christ's resurrection as well as our own! And our steadfast suffering-in-hope daily announces the present and ongoing reality of the living, risen Christ's love and mercy for his own and for this weary old world, so long at war with itself.

A Funeral Homily From 1 Thessalonians 4:13-18

Concerning the Joyful Promise of Future Resurrection

Brothers and sisters, a member of the family has died, and these flowers and our presence here today are in sympathy and celebration for our loved one and friend, who was also our brother in Christ. He blessed our lives and he finished well, not an easy accomplishment in this world which is so deeply at war with itself.

As our friend's life has taken residence beyond us, we now have cause to pause and to think about this life. We have heard much from his family. They encourage us to remember well the means by which this life touched all of us. We may find it difficult to remember our brother without also thinking of how he openly carried before us the blessed hope of the glorified future found in the Christ. This hope gave his life much of its drive and passion, especially toward the end. In fact, as much as he loved his family — and he loved all of you so very much — he lived his life with the risen Lord as his central concern.

What should be said on this particular day, then, by the pastor of such a disciple of Jesus? How should I characterize this life lived so faithfully on the Jesus-way?

To answer, I have chosen to base this funeral homily on that very familiar passage of scripture from Saint Paul's first letter to the church at Thessalonica. It is familiar to us because we often hear it read on occasions such as today. Therefore, I ask you not to allow familiarity to fog your mind. Please attend carefully to a reading of the living word of God:

> But we do not want you to be uninformed, brothers and sisters, about those who have died, so that you

may not grieve as others do who have no hope. For since we believe that Jesus died and rose again, even so, through Jesus, God will bring with him those who have died. For this we declare to you by the word of the Lord, that we who are alive, who are left until the coming of the Lord, will by no means precede those who have died. For the Lord himself, with a cry of command, with the archangel's call and with the sound of God's trumpet, will descend from heaven, and the dead in Christ will rise first. Then we who are alive, who are left, will be caught up in the clouds together with them to meet the Lord in the air; and so we will be with the Lord forever. Therefore encourage one another with these words.
— 1 Thessalonians 4:13-18

This is the word of the Lord!

Rising out of today's reading we find the primary foundation for the Christian believer's blessed hope in the Christ, the primary and foundational hope that pushes stiffly against the weight of today's grief. This underlying word comes to us from verse 14, which reads: "… since we believe that Jesus died and rose again…"

These words display, to all who care to see, the crux of the Christian faith. In fact, I am not the first to declare that everything the Christian believes and asserts hangs on the idea of Jesus' resurrection.

We could approach the text in many ways, but for the purposes dictated to us from this funeral room, there truly is but one set of questions to ask. Namely: Do we believe that Jesus vanquished the power of death by the power of the almighty God? Do we believe that Jesus openly displayed as conquered the powers of death, darkness, and empire when he absorbed evil on the cross and when he defeated evil in the resurrection? Do we believe that Jesus of Nazareth literally, physically returned to life in a resurrection body?

I simply do not know more clearly how to ask this question. Be sure of this, I do not mean the inquiry to be rhetorical. This sacred hour and this solemn room demands a literal answer from all of us.

Saint Paul gives us a clear understanding where he stood on the question. He asserts the idea of Jesus' resurrection not only as a genuinely true and historical experience, but also as the truth upon which the future of world now rests. How else could his words be taken when he writes: "For the Lord himself, with a cry of command, with the archangel's call and with the sound of God's trumpet, will descend from heaven..."?

The apostle displays to us the promise of the bodily return to earth of the resurrected Jesus — the Christ of glory — who by biblical definition is not far off somewhere in the sky, but who is actually quite literally present to us now. Take note, therefore, of how Paul's words describe Jesus' appearing as marked by power, a militant power that means to overturn the dominion of death and to set right all things in this broken world.

There will always be scoffers, those who see such reports of resurrection as, at best, mere mouthy embellishments.

Saint Peter writes about such skeptics when he says: "First of all you must understand this, that in the last days scoffers will come, scoffing and indulging their own lusts and saying, 'Where is the promise of his coming? For ever since our ancestors died, all things continue as they were from the beginning of creation!' "
— 2 Peter 3:3-4

This is why I always invite scoffers to scoff on. One day all will know the truth. One day the truth will be present again. But for now, as the scoffers scoff we lift the fallen. As they scoff we care for the dying. As they scoff we preach the peace, the hope, and the joy of a new life and a new way to live found in the living, risen Christ.

Further, we have no doubt that our brother in Christ openly believed and publicly practiced this new life and new way to live. Therefore, we have no doubt where he stood on those questions concerning resurrection, do we? His hope in life and in death stood squarely on the promise of resurrection.

That is why on this day, of all days, we rejoice in the midst of sorrow because we are able to pronounce such a clear and confident word of hope. We rejoice within the reality of this death room because we are able to announce a future beyond hospital rooms and graveyards. In fact, we are able to so announce the promise of our brother's resurrection that it produces the same professed expectation within us as it did within him! We possess a confident expectation and we encourage one another because we share his faith!

Does this mean we do not sorrow? No, without doubt we sorrow, for without doubt we know that dead is dead. Without doubt we know our brother is gone from us, at least for now. We do not question this reality. But we also know that he will not, ultimately, be held within the reality of death's grip. We know our friend in someway lives current with the presence of the Lord, sustained in a future beyond his last day with us, and even beyond this, our present day of sorrow.

Saint Paul has in mind this same confident expectation when at the beginning of today's reading he writes:

> "But we do not want you to be uninformed, brothers and sisters, about those who have died, so that

you may not grieve as others do who have no hope." And then great apostle goes on to explain: "For since we believe that Jesus died and rose again, even so, through Jesus, God will bring with him those who have died." (vv. 13-14)

Today the void cuts deep in our hearts at his passing, but brothers and sisters, our sorrow does not define us. Our sorrow does not take us beyond the bounds of this confident expectation found in the Lord which we describe today. Therefore, let us take the apostle's council. Let us allow our grief to run its full course, but never as those who have no hope, never to the point of despair.

As the great apostle asserts, those who die in the Lord are held by the strength of life found from that same risen Jesus, and even now they prevail in his presence. Likewise, those who die in the Lord — on that day of days when the hidden and present kingdom becomes visible and fully realized — will return with the Lord to this place then reclaimed and remade as God always intended, and so shall we, together again, ever be with the Lord!

Let us then comfort each other with this blessed hope. And let us remind each other in these coming days of sorrow, when we seek our friend and find him gone, that gone is not forever and gone is not the final word. Amen.

A Funeral Homily From 2 Corinthians 1

Concerning the God of Mercy and Consolation

Our gathering together on this day and in this place forces us to confront the truth that our brother in Christ no longer lives with us. We congregate here because of the importance found in acknowledging to ourselves and to the watching world that our friend lived among us, he blessed us with his presence, and he left us to be with the Lord whom he loved. Therefore, it is completely appropriate and even necessary that we should gather in this way.

But let us be clear, our brother left us too suddenly and too soon, and therefore we now endure suffering. We can rejoice that he will be found in the presence of the Lord, and we believe that he will never again be separated from the living, risen Christ, but brothers and sisters, we who remain behind must face a future without him, at least for a time. This separation hits us where we live and opens in us a very deep grief.

Therefore, my desire today as your pastor is to bring a word of encouragement. I hope to offer council from the heart of the Christian faith, expressing comfort, especially as we face this future of separation. To this end I would ask you to attend to a reading from chapter 1 of Saint Paul's second letter to the churches located in the Mediterranean city of Corinth. As we shall see, it is a text that inhales comfort and exhales hope. Saint Paul writes:

> Blessed be the God and Father of our Lord Jesus Christ, the Father of mercies and the God of all consolation, who consoles us in all our affliction, so that we may be able to console those who are in any

affliction with the consolation with which we ourselves are consoled by God. For just as the sufferings of Christ are abundant for us, so also our consolation is abundant through Christ. If we are being afflicted, it is for your consolation and salvation; if we are being consoled, it is for your consolation, which you experience when you patiently endure the same sufferings that we are also suffering. Our hope for you is unshaken; for we know that as you share in our sufferings, so also you share in our consolation.
— 2 Corinthians 1:3-7

This is the word of the Lord!
Notice from the outset of the reading how the holy scripture more than acknowledges the existence of the human condition. That is, far from downplaying the reality of this brutal world at war with itself, the Bible in general and here Saint Paul specifically accepts the concreteness of the complete brokenness of God's good creation. We see this in the reading when the great apostle describes the chaos of the human condition by using the word "affliction," as in, "who consoles us in all our affliction." This word brings to mind any number of human troubles. In fact, this word "affliction" can mean distress, oppression, tribulation, and even the pressure that comes from being compressed or crushed. Today, we know personally this affliction, do we not? We know what it means to be heart-crushed. We know the tribulation that comes from the death of a loved one and friend.
At first, therefore, we should be glad for the Bible's acknowledgement of the truth of the affliction found within the human condition. By being honest with us concerning the death, the grief, the hate, the greed, and the violence that seems now to run free in the world, the scriptures are able to honestly speak truth to those, who like us, grieve and suffer. I do not know how I would be able to stand before you this

day if I were forced to speak words from a book that pretended we did not live in such an awful mess! Thankfully, I am not forced to do so.

However, if this is all the Bible has to say to us, that the world is a mess and we, ourselves, have only succeeded in making it worse, then, truly, what good is that? I mean, after nearly forty years of ministry, you can imagine how many hospital rooms, nursing homes, and graveyards through which I have been forced to walk. And, sadly, your experiences are no doubt much the same. If this is all the Bible has to say, that we are broken and live among a broken people, well, let's just pack the tents and go home.

But you know as well as I do that the holy scriptures bring to us much more than this. The Bible does not leave us alone within the darkness of this broken world but also brings us comfort with the truth of a divine consolation. Listen again to a portion of Saint Paul's teaching: "Blessed be the God and Father of our Lord Jesus Christ, the Father of mercies and the God of all consolation, who consoles us in all our affliction…"

Notice how the apostle refers to the almighty as "the Father of mercies and the God of all consolation." We learn through this designation that the Lord comes with reassurance and compassion in the midst of our deepening distress. We learn that God shows a kindness and a forbearance in affliction, even to those who do not deserve such consideration. In the end that would mean all of us!

We still may wonder whether this divine mercy would apply to us, especially on this day. Does such consolation cover the heartache found in this death room? Very much so. Today, the Lord offers this very promise of compassionate help that the great apostle describes. In fact, today the Lord brings himself to us as the one who stands up to our sorrow, desiring our daily healing, if we will allow him to do so, but how?

To be sure, we want this healing to descend upon us, but where should we look? From which direction will it come to us?

First, we must understand that the "how" of consolation comes from discerning the "who" of consolation. As you know, the New Testament was originally written in the Greek language. The word in today's reading translated "consolation" comes from the Greek word *paraklēseōs* — that literally means, "the one who is called alongside to help." What is important to note is that this word *paraklēseōs* is the same form of the word used to describe the Holy Spirit in Saint John's gospel. That is, when Jesus promises his disciples that another "comforter" would come to them after he ascended to his heavenly Father, it is a form of this same word.

Brothers and sisters, that we would hear the depth of this truth. You see, as followers of the Jesus-way we now know the reality of Jesus' promise fulfilled. We now know this Comforter as the one who inhabits our lives and who always brings to us this promised consolation, comfort, and mercy from the almighty God. We now know this Comforter as the one who is moment-by-moment called alongside to help us through our affliction. We now know the Comforter as the Holy Spirit.

Think of the comforting work of the Holy Spirit in this way. The death of our friend hits us hard. It knocks the wind from us. We lie flattened on the ground, so much so that suffering leaks from us like blood from a wound. Suddenly, the Comforter is summoned to our side, offering his help and saying, "Here, let me bandage you; let me help you up. I know you are weak; I know you are flesh. Let me help you up." We consent, and as we offer ourselves to the Holy Spirit a fresh breath comes to our spirit and a new toughness strengthens our weary soul. We stand. Then grief rushes back and in a few moments we again fall under the weight of sorrow. Swiftly, the almighty summons the comforting Holy

Spirit to our side and the process begins all over again. The Comforter works toward us in this way.

But there is more. Not only does the Comforter come beside us, but those who have been comforted by the Holy Spirit through their affliction now stand beside us as well. Remember, Saint Paul also writes: "Father of mercies and the God of all consolation... consoles us in all our affliction, so that we may be able to console those who are in any affliction with the consolation with which we ourselves are consoled by God" (vv. 3-4).

That is, those who have been comforted become a conduit of comfort for others now afflicted. We experience the consolation and mercy from the Lord and then we must pass that same consolation and that same mercy to the one beside us who lays crumbled on the ground. This describes how the body of the living, risen Christ — the church — stands together through the present suffering of the human condition, and through the present suffering in this funeral room.

Know this: One day our faith will be made sight. One day — on that day of days — we will see the triumph of the Lord and his kingdom when all things will be set right, when all people who want to be with the Lord will be with him, and when all the world will become just what the almighty God always intended. However, this kingdom has not yet been realized and so now we continue to suffer, but just as real as our present anguish is the present reality of our standing side-by-side with the Holy Spirit and with each other. We suffer together. We stand beside each other as co-comforters with the almighty and the Holy Spirit, and together we lift each other up from the broken shards of loss, returning one another — moment by moment — to our proper places of hope and grace.

A Funeral Homily From Isaiah 40:27-31

Concerning the Death of Someone Unknown to the Pastor

Today grief gathers around us as a stormy sea, moving over us in waves of suffering. It does not bring us much help to understand that we share these same feelings of loss with all the wounded and grieving around the world, does it? That today's funeral service is not the only funeral service does not impress because we find it difficult to turn our minds toward anything other than our own suffering. It would be surprising if it were to happen any other way. True grief always captures our full attention.

Therefore, I consider it an honor to be with you today to help you grieve and to encourage you through your sadness. I want you to know that I take my vocation from the Lord with utmost seriousness, and I truly hope to contribute God's comforting word toward you with care and honesty.

To help me accomplish this calling, I will base this funeral homily upon a scripture from the Hebrew Bible, a scripture that will offer us a wisdom beyond our own. If your heart sorrows and desires to hear hope-filled enlightenment, it will be presented through the discernment of the prophet Isaiah, who brings to us the word of the Lord as found in chapter 40 of his prophecy. Please attend now to a reading of the living word of God:

> Why do you say, O Jacob, and speak, O Israel, "My way is hidden from the Lord, and my right is disregarded by my God"? Have you not known? Have you not heard? The Lord is the everlasting God, the Creator of the ends of the earth. He does not faint or grow weary; his understanding is unsearchable. He

gives power to the faint, and strengthens the powerless. Even youths will faint and be weary, and the young will fall exhausted; but those who wait for the Lord shall renew their strength, they shall mount up with wings like eagles, they shall run and not be weary, they shall walk and not faint.
— Isaiah 40:27-31

This is the word of the Lord!

The prophet Isaiah's original audience for this reading — the ancient Hebrews — endured the loss of their nation, the death of their loved ones, and the plunder of their possessions. In their minds even the promises of God failed them because all these events eventually resulted in their bitter exile to a foreign country. In confusion and despair, hope finally escaped from their hearts. Grief reigned.

Given these historical circumstances, surely these ancient words from God rush toward us today and toward the suffering faced in this room. That is, God has something to say to us because grief reigns here as well.

To understand God's word for us today, therefore, let us first notice how the text begins with questions. In our grief through loss we most often put God on the witness stand, do we not? We most often feel compelled to ask searing questions of the almighty, wanting a detailed account as to why this event happened or why that happening occurred. But today's reading actually makes something of a peculiar twist. Today's text turns the tables on those ancient Hebrews, and by extension we experience this turning as well. You see, Isaiah tells us that God asks the questions and we must give the response. Here the text reads:

Why do you say, O Jacob, and speak, O Israel, "My way is hidden from the Lord, and my right is disregarded by my God"?

God questions: "Why do you say I no longer see you? Why do you speak as if I no longer regard your life? Why do you live as if I have forgotten you?"

Grief feels just like this, does it not? Grief shuts us down and closes us off from others and even from ourselves. Grief takes us out into the deep waters where we can easily believe ourselves alone in the watery winds of the chaos that comprises the human condition. Like those ancient Hebrews, we can easily believe ourselves forsaken by God. But this is a most important point: The fact that we feel this way does not necessarily make this feeling true, does it?

In fact, God's questions to those ancient Hebrews were meant to lead them to this very understanding — that they were not at all abandoned as they feared themselves to be. To be sure, chaos lurks just below the surface of the human condition, but does it follow because the chaos hits us where we live that God indeed has forgotten us? Is this truly what we believe? If so, Isaiah offers God's response:

> Have you not known? Have you not heard? The Lord is the everlasting God, the Creator of the ends of the earth. He does not faint or grow weary; his understanding is unsearchable.
> (v. 28)

It is as if the Lord says, "Hear me! I do not grow weary. I do not give up or give in. I have not lost my way, therefore, I have not forgotten you! But you simply cannot understand what I know, for I see what cannot be seen!"

Here, the ever-present God speaks through his prophet with providential words of care, reminding his people of their place in the world. You see, the Lord desires to provoke his people so that they find within their hearts this profound and deep-seated truth: They still stand subject to God's love and God's purposes even in their suffering, which he will ultimately turn toward their good and toward the ultimate good.

Isaiah does not mean to say that God affirms all things good or that all happenings are his will. Far from it. But he does mean for us to know that God's ever-presence brings to us a reality beyond the present chaos. Allow me to repeat this because it is of utmost importance: God's ever-presence brings us a reality beyond the present chaos. The Lord through Isaiah explains himself, in this regard:

> He gives power to the faint, and strengthens the powerless. Even youths will faint and be weary, and the young will fall exhausted; but those who wait for the Lord shall renew their strength, they shall mount up with wings like eagles, they shall run and not be weary, they shall walk and not faint.
> (vv. 29-31)

This final portion of the reading, then, closes in on the deepest of truths by declaring to us that God has not forgotten us as we supposed, not at all. In fact, God never abandons us, but we must be careful that we do not abandon God.

This means that while we feel lost because we live within the consequences of our free-will choices and within the chaos of the human condition, God calls us to choose faith, anyway, no matter how we feel. God calls us to believe that he remains with his people, ever and always. God calls us to see that he is with his people and truly acts in favor toward them, giving them the daily strength they need to be sustained in this arduous journey.

"Those who wait for the Lord shall renew their strength," reads the text, and now we arrive at the heart of wisdom from the Hebrew prophet. Now we hear announced the reality of God's renewing strength, a strength given to those willing to admit powerlessness and those willing to wait for God's help to surge in them.

God consistently acts in love toward us, but there are conditions in our discovering those actions: We must admit our need and we must wait for divine help to apprehend us. But just how difficult this admission and this waiting is for us.

Ask of us anything else, Lord, but do not ask us to confess weakness, and especially, do not ask us to wait! Often our response to this calling from the Lord goes something like this: "Where are you God; don't you see us? We hurt, now! Loss rips us apart, now! We want deliverance, now!"

But the prophet counsels us to wait on the Lord. Do not doubt the Lord's goodness, wait for the Lord's unsearchable peace to surface beside you.

Wait on the Lord! Expect his strength to well up in your hearts and quite suddenly he will express strength to you.

Wait on the Lord! Break open your anger, insuring it does not fester into a bitterness that poisons your soul.

Wait on the Lord! Allow these overwhelming feelings of sadness to rush in waves over your heart, knowing that genuine healing only emerges through these surges of suffering.

Wait on the Lord! Wait with a heart filled with a tension that causes you to wonder, "Will I survive?" Yes, you will if you squarely face your grief.

So wait, I say, wait on the Lord, and to your utter surprise, you will discover that almighty God was with you in this sea of grief all along, holding you above the bitter waves by the love found in the sheer strength of his grace.

A Funeral Homily From John 13

Concerning a Death from Suicide

Who would believe the dreadful events of this week just past? Who would believe the emotional trauma this family and this church family have been made to withstand? Few life events dislocate us like death, and with perhaps the exception of the death of a child, few actions offer more of death's dislocation to a community than when someone takes their own life.

The events of this week now bring us to this place and to this hour. As we gather here, huddled together in confusion, anger, and regret we ask question after question, but we receive no answers. We think about what if we had said this or what if we had done that, would it have made a difference? We simply do not know.

As a Christian church, as his church, we feel many emotions. We feel guilty because we sense we may have let down our loved one and friend. To be sure, for a very long time we knew he struggled but we did not realize his isolation; we did not realize the depth of his despair. Guilt is not our only emotion. We also feel anger. We feel anger at ourselves; we feel anger at him. How could this happen? How could he do this without leaving a word? But mostly and especially we feel responsible; we feel we should have been there for him. Had we only known; had we only looked to see. Perhaps we were too busy. Perhaps we missed the signs. Perhaps he did not signal his fractured spirit. Perhaps he was unable to do so.

As his family, I cannot imagine your hurt. I am sure you find your feelings crash-landing all over the place. Your tears and anger and remorse are quite normal, and much time will be needed to heal this wound because I am confident your confusion must seem to deepen with each passing hour.

What can we do? What can be done? Whatever we do, I am convinced that it must be done together. Whatever we do, we must somehow retie the bonds that Christ gives us for days such as this. Whatever we do, we must encourage our damaged hearts to heal and our affection for life to return. And whatever else we do, we must somehow learn to walk this confusing road of sorrow within the healing body of the living, risen Christ.

What can be said to help us? What words can be offered to enable us to walk this confusing road? In moments such as this I find genuine help when I turn to holy scripture. The scriptures speak heartfelt truth to us with a power that allows us to see through the present calamity into the very presence of God. Holy scripture mediates the reality of God to our spirits so that we eventually learn we do not travel this way of tears by ourselves.

To this end, I have decided to base my very brief remarks for today's funeral homily on the words of Jesus from Saint John's gospel, chapter 13. Attend now, therefore, to a reading of the living word of God:

> I give you a new commandment, that you love one another. Just as I have loved you, you also should love one another. By this everyone will know that you are my disciples, if you have love for one another.
> — John 13:34-35

This is the gospel of the Lord!

This text offers us a solid reminder that we, each of us, possess a deep calling on our lives from the Lord. This text also serves to remind us that, if the Lord's calling on our lives means anything, it means, supremely, that we owe the ministry of loving service toward one another.

Hear then my message for this suffering family and for the broken-hearted forever-family that is this church: In the wake of this tragic death, let us sincerely go about the business of loving one another.

This is what must be done.

To that end, then, let us lay aside every petty difference and let us love one another. Let us lay aside the sins and the weights that prevent us from doing the Lord's will and instead let us seek to practice love toward one another, for I am convinced that as we face this dire hour nothing else matters and nothing less will help.

To truly love one another means we first must feel the full weight of our brother's soul's disorder. We must allow the weight of his despair to fully come upon us. And we must allow ourselves to hear — in the echo of our brother's final cry of discouragement — a call to help the afflicted other beside us. We take on this weight so that we do our best never again to miss the signs of desperation. Here we pray, "O Lord, give us ears to hear and hearts to understand."

There is more. In Jesus' command to love one another I want you to take note how we must go about this task. We must love each other with Jesus' love — "Just as I have loved you, you also should love one another," says the Lord.

What could this kind of loving one another mean? Strangely enough, in context, it means foot washing. Just before he spoke these words Jesus had taken the form of a bond-servant and washed the disciples' feet. Jesus willingly disregarded his position as leader and the personal power that dictated others must serve him. Instead, he freely pushed all this away from himself and, in an act of sacrificial love that would lead to reconciling forgiveness, he knelt before his followers and functioned as a household slave.

This is what it means to truly love one another, it means to serve one another.

We would be wise to take note that this instance of helping and humility was not the only instance that Jesus lived before us. Think of how his place on the cross displayed this same position of a servant. The cross placed Jesus in the position of the criminal — the despised and the rejected. The cross placed Jesus in the position of chosen weakness. Little did the ones viewing these events discern the power behind his embodiment of sacrificial love! Jesus chose this position of service. This is the Jesus-way, and this is what his calling on our lives means, to love one another.

But even this is not all. To truly love one another through the Jesus-way of sacrificial love means we must see the other in a particular way. In Jesus' command to love one another I always hear echoes of the Bible question found in the Hebrew Bible: "Am I my brother's keeper?"

How would you answer?

I believe we must reply, "Yes, we really are responsible, we really are our brother's and sister's keepers." I would argue that this "keeping" project is the essence of the Christian practice of a sacrificial service that truly follows the Jesus-way.

This means our calling demands we respond to our responsibility to stand side-by-side with those whom the Lord brings our way. This means our calling insists we stand side-by-side with the dispossessed ones, allowing their heart-ruptured cry to sound on us, so that their grief is captured in our hearts as well.

One way we could describe this "keeping" of the other would be as the ministry of absorption. Following the example of the Lord himself, we "keep" our brother or sister by willingly absorbing their brokenness. You see, if this truly is a forever-family in more than name only, we must be unafraid to accept the un-antiseptic risk. We must not become weary in well-doing, but instead we must open ourselves to the on-going pain of this community, absorbing it in love and in Jesus' name.

We could describe this "keeping" of the other as the ministry of acceptance. That is, and again following the example of the Lord, we accept people just as they are, without asking them to reach our standards before we love and forgive them. The Lord, after all, accepts us, loves us, and forgives us. Who are we not to approach those in need in the same way?

The consequence of this means we all must stand together in this mess. No one bears exemption from offering care and love for this broken family seated here and for this hurting forever-family.

Finally, I would say to this suffering family sitting before me, there is something important for you to do. You must let us love you. You must let down your guard and let us into the world of hurt, anger, and perhaps even the world of shame you now feel. You must let us obey the Lord by standing vigil with you and carrying the burdens with you. This is our calling from the Lord and this is how you will discover that the Lord himself stands very close to you in this hour of great sorrow.

A Funeral Homily From Psalm 13

Concerning the Death of a Child

We should not be here today. These parents should not be burying their child — no parent should have to do this, and this church should not be made to bear the suffering from the death of one of our little ones. Yet, here we stand.

We might begin by asking just what, if anything, can be said on this occasion. What do you suppose that I can say as the pastor of this church and of this little one that would make any difference at all? In response I must answer, there is nothing. I can say nothing at all that will absorb the grief stains from our hearts. This mountain of anguish rises much too high for my words to scale.

There remains, therefore, only one righteous response to the calamity of this hour, and that response is to plainly tell each other the truth. In fact, in this hour we must hear the utmost honesty proclaimed, for no other pathway will offer even the slightest possibility of leading us away from the abyss.

Bromides and axioms just will not cut it, not on this day. Well-meaning people tend to mouth clichés that seek to turn away the grief, but only from themselves, so they do not feel the pain of the broken-hearted one before them. What else could it mean when someone says, "Well, God wanted another angel" or "It was her time"? We will have none of that now, not here, not as we keep vigil in this sacred place of suffering.

What truth needs to be told? Quite simply this day is wrong. It is brutal and hateful. This day shatters the illusion of business as usual. This day throws our understanding of the world out of balance. This day we are angry. This day we are afflicted. This day we doubt all we were taught. This day we simply cannot make the pain go away; we cannot sprinkle the usual religious incantations so that we do not feel cheated and wrongfully used. This day nothing works.

But this truth is about as far as we know to go. More needs to be said. We need more truth spoken but we do not have it within ourselves. Thankfully, there does abide in our possession the exact words we need to express the truth of our outrage and grief. These words spring forth from the Hebrew poets who brought before the almighty — through the gift of their creativity and the pain of their suffering — words of protest and complaint. We call these worship poems the psalms of lament, and they comprise the largest genre of poetry in the psalter.

For our grief work today, therefore, I will read one of these psalms — number 13. As I proclaim the poem I would challenge all of us to find within its words the lesions of grief that now discharge sorrow from our own wounded spirits.

Therefore, as best as you are able, attend to a reading of the living word of God:

> How long, O Lord? Will you forget me forever? How long will you hide your face from me? How long must I bear pain in my soul, and have sorrow in my heart all day long? How long shall my enemy be exalted over me? Consider and answer me, O Lord my God! Give light to my eyes, or I will sleep the sleep of death, and my enemy will say, "I have prevailed"; my foes will rejoice because I am shaken. But I trusted in your steadfast love; my heart shall rejoice in your salvation. I will sing to the Lord, because he has dealt bountifully with me.
> — Psalm 13:1-6

We thank the poet for speaking for us, voicing to God the truth from our wounded hearts. We thank the poet for opening before us the deep crevices of sorrow, exposing them to the clear light of day and the healing of holy scripture. Since we now have this opening, let us think through two ideas from the text, which will then present a path for me to address our church — the discipleship community where this little one called home, and her dear, suffering family.

First, to the text. Notice how the poet laments in the clearest of complaints: "How long, O Lord? Will you forget me forever? How long will you hide your face from me?" (v. 1). The poet's questions echo both Psalm 22 and the cry of dereliction from Jesus himself, when from the cross he shouted: "My God, my God, why have you forsaken me?"

This lament opens one of the believer's primary concerns: God, where are you? When trouble captures us and shakes our foundations, where are you? But the questioning does not stop there. No, the poet is relentless in his pursuit of answers, saying: "How long must I bear pain in my soul, and have sorrow in my heart all day long?" (v. 2).

What are we to say? As to the first question, "Where is God?" I respond: God is present. God's reality is current, side-by-side with us, and I declare to you that when this little one drifted away from us, God was the first to weep.

"But," you say, "God should have saved her!"

And I respond, just her? Surely not just her! What about all the other little girls being buried by all the other grieving families all around the world today, and even at this very hour? What about them?

No, we must tell the truth, remember? Here we are forced to understand the reality of the human condition. We are born and we die, and along the way we struggle. I have been in the Christian ministry for nearly forty years, and I can count very few times when I truly believed that the miraculous occurred and the almighty thwarted the way of the world. I understand what other clergy say in this regard, but remember, from the outset we determined to tell ourselves the truth.

We must also understand that God almighty is not our personal caretaker. God is not our Santa Claus, doling out protection if we attend this many services of worship or so many classes of Sunday learning. Our relationship with the almighty just does not work this way. No, God is God, and we are not. God is mystery and our finite minds can only approximate who God is and what God does. This we do know: God does not kill little girls. God does not seek to ruin lives. Or, as he himself says through the prophet Jeremiah: "For surely I know the plans I have for you, says the Lord, plans for your welfare and not for harm, to give you a future with hope" (Jeremiah 29:11).

At this point it will help to take careful note how the poem ends. It does not end with questions, although the questions remain. Instead it ends with faith: "But I trusted in your steadfast love; my heart shall rejoice in your salvation. I will sing to the Lord, because he has dealt bountifully with me," says the poet (vv. 5-6).

The pain? Still present. The grief? Still relentless. But beside the pain and grief stands strong the faith in final salvation and the song of joy at the Lord's unending bounty.

Clearly, we are not ready to take this faith to heart, not yet, for we are too dazed, too numb. That brings the poem's second question to the front: "How long must I bear pain in my soul, and have sorrow in my heart all day long?" (v. 2).

How long, indeed? When will this suffering end? When will we be able to rejoice in the salvation from the Lord so that we are able to again sing of the almighty's bounty? How long before we move forward from here, from this room that now captures our hearts?

In response to how long, I want to address our church, this discipleship community, and then I want to follow that by offering a word to the family because if we can find a way to grieve together, we can eventually find a way to the sunlight.

First, to our Church:

Do Not Offer Advice. The temptation will be to help this dear family with many words of counsel. Do not go there. In fact, do not speak much of anything. Instead, allow your silent witness to demonstrate your love. Be close. Be present. Be sensitive. Be active in your care, but share your love not your thoughts.

Be a Listener. In the months to come, much of our pain at this loss will dissipate, but it will not be so for this family. How long must they "bear pain in their soul, and have sorrow in their heart all day long"? asks the poet, and we answer that they will grieve for a very, very long time. In many ways they will grieve forever. Therefore, give them the gift of listening. Allow them to grieve, allow them to cry, and allow them to share their story — which is really *our* story — by receiving their loss and absorbing their sorrow over and over again. This listening comprises the true heart-work of this community of faith.

Speak of This Child. I realize this is counterintuitive, but it will greatly help alleviate sorrow when we remember and mention this little one to each other and especially to her family. We love her and to bring her memory forward to each other and to her loved ones, while causing tears, I assure you will advance a wealth of comfort.

Second, to the Family:

Do Not Succumb to Solitude. Grief demands that we mourn alone. Grief shuts us off from each other, from the loved and known. Grief insists that we move to the shadow so that no one sees our ordeal. Do not allow this to happen.

Come clean. What is the worst that can happen? You might cry in front of us. You might fall apart. So what? We love you; we stand with you. Let us cry with you.

Invite the Lord to Help. The Lord will help. He has willingly taken on the task of shepherding his people. Choose to allow him to stand beside you as you suffer. Daily trust your suffering to the reassuring grace of the almighty, allowing your sorrow to flow to his safekeeping. Make the decision, now; ask for his care.

Invite Us to Help. Do not block the church's concern. This will be very difficult, but receive our care. You are members of this forever-family and together we have resources that you alone now no longer possess. For example, it may be a long time before you are able to pray again in any meaningful way. Do not worry about this; let us intercede for you. This is our work now. We walk the road of sorrow with you, and in this special way we walk it for you.

Remember the Future. Do not think that this mess holds before you the final word. This little one's story does not end here! I would proclaim to you, on the authority of the living word of God, that even now we rush forward toward a moment when our faith will be sight, when hope will be realized, and when grace will say a final amen over the brutality of this world.

On that day, when we are again reunited with our beautiful child and with all of God's people, we will discover, to our utter amazement, that everything lost here will be restored tenfold in that place of reclamation and recovery. So do not lose heart; do not grieve as those who have no hope.

Or as Saint Paul wrote: "So we do not lose heart. Even though our outer nature is wasting away, our inner nature is being renewed day by day. For this slight momentary affliction is preparing us for an eternal weight of glory beyond all measure, because we look not at what can be seen but at what cannot be seen; for what can be seen is temporary, but what cannot be seen is eternal" (2 Corinthians 4:16-18).

To which we say, "Amen, and Amen. May God be with us."

A Funeral Homily From Psalm 46

Concerning the God of Refuge and Strength

I have chosen to base today's funeral homily upon Psalm 46. This psalm contains such a compelling word of encouragement that I offer it today because I often find myself inhabiting this poem, running its meaning through my heart as a way to find my own gravity, especially when the earth shakes under my feet and when the solid mountains seem to be shattering into the sea.

This psalm pulses with life and it infuses hope because it reminds us of God's self-imposed obligation to love his world all the way to the end. Therefore, let us attend to this reading of the living word of God, asking in its hearing for the God who is our healer to embody the text and to comfort us through it:

> God is our refuge and strength, a very present help in trouble. Therefore we will not fear, though the earth should change, though the mountains shake in the heart of the sea; though its waters roar and foam, though the mountains tremble with its tumult. *Selah* There is a river whose streams make glad the city of God, the holy habitation of the Most High. God is in the midst of the city; it shall not be moved; God will help it when the morning dawns. The nations are in an uproar, the kingdoms totter; he utters his voice, the earth melts. The Lord of hosts is with us; the God of Jacob is our refuge. *Selah* Come, behold the works of the Lord; see what desolations he has brought on the earth. He makes wars cease to the end of the earth; he breaks the bow, and shatters the spear; he burns the

shields with fire. "Be still, and know that I am God! I am exalted among the nations, I am exalted in the earth." The Lord of hosts is with us; the God of Jacob is our refuge. *Selah*
— Psalm 46

A good way into the psalm text for our purposes in this sad hour is to ask just what the psalmist means to tell us about the world in his poem. He clearly means to remind us of what we already know: the earth changes, the mountains shake and fall into the heart of the sea; the waters roar and foam, the mountains tremble with tumult.

What does this mean? It means we live in chaos. We live under the constant threat of trouble. But I need not convince you of this reality, do I? You live the chaos right now. Today you know by experience the shaking tumult that accompanies the death of your loved one and friend. You are in the very heart of the darkness that is the grief of loss.

I always seek to warn our people where I pastor, if you are not in trouble, then you are headed there! You may be on top of the mountain, but sooner or later the mountain will be on top of you!

Is this pessimism or realism? Perhaps a little of both. I do know that I have far too often walked the halls of nursing homes, hospitals, and funeral homes, and more than I care to think about I have walked over the marble stones and the green grass of graveyards.

This is reality and I tell you it does us no good to pretend. It does us no good to fail to see the world as it truly is, broken and in trouble. But it also does us no good to think that chaos is all there is of the world. This fails the truth as well.

No, chaos often presents itself to us, but stands as only one half of the story! God's presence stands as the other half, and here the text shines with hope: "God is our refuge and strength, a very present help in trouble" (v. 1). And then later on the poet promises: "God is in the midst of the city; it shall not be moved" (v. 5).

Here then is the lesson: God is our refuge; God is in our midst. God is the strength and shelter from the chaos of falling mountains, and this God shall not be moved. Yes, this God is our strength when calamity crushes us.

I truly love the statement: "God is a very present help in trouble." This may be the most important announcement in holy scripture. God is present, his Spirit with us, and he sees our trouble and invites us to run to him. He calls on us to run to him as shelter and as refuge.

And finally because God is present, the poet tells us, "… we will not fear." The old-timers would call a statement like this a "great and precious promise."

Sadly, it seems to me that so much of the time we live our lives in fear, but here the poet wants us to see that fearfulness wastes our life because anxiety steals our days and our energy. Are we condemned to this fear? No, we are not; we are given a choice. We may choose to live without fear because God's presence sustains us, strengthens us, and shelters us. This mourning which you now experience truly is a storm, make no mistake about it, but you may run to the shelter and strength of the Lord who comforts and sustains so that you come through the fear.

But you say, "Preacher, I called on the Lord, and I have not heard a thing! Where is this shelter?"

Yes, I know; I am well aware of this problem. Here again the text helps when the poet encourages us by saying: "Be still, and know that I am God! I am exalted among the nations, I am exalted in the earth."

Be still and know! Be still? How can I be still? I am broken. This burden of loss crushed me. How can I be still?

Being still may not be as difficult as you think. Being still simply means we change our focus. We choose to turn from our brokenness and this crushing burden — real and powerful as it is — and instead we focus on the Lord, who moment by moment willingly brings us peace. We freely choose to see the one, who through the chaos lives forever as our loving heavenly Father. We volunteer our hearts to focus on the one who promises to walk this weary road with us and to provide us each day exactly what we need.

Perhaps you are thinking, "But, preacher, I'm not there yet. I don't know if I can change focus." Yes, I know. All you really have to do is pray this prayer: "Lord, help me." That is, pour out your grief and burden before the Lord by this modest request for help, and this prayer will take you to his shelter; this prayer will bring to you his strength.

Do not expect angels to sing or lightning to flash. Do not expect anything really. Just wait. Just linger over the prayer, offering it over and over again every time the grief slams you down into the dust. Then suddenly you will notice a strange, subtle sense of strength growing. Not that the tumult will end. No, the trouble will still be present, storming around, but the almighty's presence will be there as well. The almighty will give you shelter and under that shield who is the God of all comfort, you will find amplified within your heart this certain, unexplainable sound of peace.

A Funeral Homily From Hebrews 4

Concerning the Death of a Young Person by Accident

I have chosen to base my remarks for today's funeral homily upon a passage of holy scripture found in the book of Hebrews, chapter 4. It is a text that inhales comfort and exhales hope.

I offer this particular text to you on this particularly difficult day because it genuinely voices what needs to be communicated to us. It is a brief passage of scripture, only 84 words, but as I say, it is unusually dense with power and meaning. I also offer this passage to you because these biblical words not only bring to our minds thoughts that carry comfort and grace — which we desperately need — but they also deliver a truth which helps to explain the reality of how we live in a world so ordered where velocity, gravity, and physics can coalesce and collide and suddenly snatch 26 year olds from us without warning!

Let us begin our grief work by giving these ancient words an attentive hearing, finding in them both truth and hope for this moment of great need. Attend now, to a reading of the living word of God:

> Since, then, we have a great high priest who has passed through the heavens, Jesus, the Son of God, let us hold fast to our confession. For we do not have a high priest who is unable to sympathize with our weaknesses, but we have one who in every respect has been tested as we are, yet without sin. Let us therefore approach the throne of grace with boldness, so that we may receive mercy and find grace to help in time of need.
> — Hebrews 4:14-16

This is the word of the Lord!

Notice first how the holy scripture portrays the living, risen Jesus as being our great high priest. The text reads: "Since, then, we have a great high priest who has passed through the heavens, Jesus, the Son of God..." (v. 14).

This is a most interesting and an exceedingly helpful way to describe the Christ as our great high priest, the living Jesus functions as our mediator with God, the holy Father. That is, the Christ takes the almighty's love and mercy and, even in the midst of all our shock and sorrow, he lavishes it upon our broken hearts. But this is not all. The Christ also brings our brokenness and our hollowed-out hearts before the almighty, translating the groans of our pain — which lie so deep within us that they cannot even be uttered intelligibly — and he translates them back to the God who is there and who is not silent.

It is important that we dig a little deeper into the meaning of Jesus' priesthood. Clearly, the writer of today's text means to explain the truth of God's love for us when we read: "... we do not have a high priest who is unable to sympathize with our weaknesses, but we have one who in every respect has been tested..." (v. 15).

That is, the living and risen Christ, who is Jesus of Nazareth, and who himself experienced the very deep brokenness of the human condition through his own incarnation, now grants to the almighty God — the one who exists as the very foundation of the world — a thorough understanding of our weaknesses, our brokenness, and our grief. This even includes the brutality of today's tears. That means we can never shake our finger in the face of the almighty and accuse, "You do not understand! You do not care!" These fears are simply untrue.

Okay, we get it. God understands. Well and good, but at this grave occasion we must also ask, so what? What does this change? What should we do with this overwhelming burden of grief we still carry, even if it is carried under God's understanding?

The text answers this question when it brings before us two vital responses to the calamity of the human condition such as we now experience in all its brutality. First, we are told to: "hold fast to our confession." To hold fast to our confession means we hold fast to the confession that Jesus is Lord, and it means we hold fast to the confession that the world ultimately makes sense, even if we walk in chaos now.

"... hold fast to our confession..."

Of course, this is easier said than done. In our brokenness from loss we may naturally question why things happen the way they do. Then we realize that freewill is built into the warp and woof of the human being; we realize that human beings make choices which cause ripples that never cease; and we realize that our God is not the cause of evil and is instead our ultimate ground of support and comfort.

Or we could say it the way the Hebrew poet did in today's psalm reading:

> I lift up my eyes to the hills — from where will my help come? My help comes from the Lord, who made heaven and earth. He will not let your foot be moved; he who keeps you will not slumber. He who keeps Israel will neither slumber nor sleep.
> — Psalm 121:1-4

The Hebrew poet asks, "from where will my help come?" and then answers his own question: "My help comes from the Lord, who made heaven and earth." All of these thoughts finally lead us to realize that our true calling during this present suffering becomes the daily choice of faith. We either choose to stand firm in faith, even though we bear the burden of a shredded heart, or we choose not to so stand.

To be sure, the choice of faith I am describing recognizes the reality of the brokenness of life. This choice for faith fully labors under the deep heartache of the human condition, but chooses to believe anyway. This choice for faith decides daily — or perhaps moment by moment — to believe that God is good, that God is present to us, and finally that God cares what happens in this world and in our world.

But this is not all. As I said the text also brings to light a second vital response to the brutality of the human condition. You see, standing in faith doesn't mean standing in meekness or worse yet standing in silence. Here the text delivers us to the very heart of comfort when we read: "… approach the throne of grace with boldness, so that we may receive mercy and find grace to help in time of need."

Through our great high priest — the living, risen Christ — the way for mercy, the way for help and the way for grace stands thrown wide open. Access to the God of all mercy stands clear and open before us, all we must do is enter.

I asked before, what do we do with this burden of grief we carry? We hold to the confession of our faith and then we carry this burden before the Lord who loves us. How are we to come before the almighty? The text reads: "Let us therefore approach the throne of grace with boldness…" (v. 16).

Boldness. This word boldness can also be translated, "with confidence." This takes the idea of boldness beyond brashness to the notion of assurance. We can come before the almighty, bringing with us the reality our brokenness, but we need not do so with timidity. Instead we approach the Lord with the full confidence that he hears and understands. We approach the Lord by faith, believing that he constantly moves toward us in mercy and believing that he constantly understands the reality of our sufferings.

Here we find the very heart of our suffering exposed. You see, grief runs away. Grief makes us seek the solitude and the shadows and not the Lord. Grief desires to walk alone, to remain unseen by the watching world. But the text calls for a different response. The text calls for us to leave the shadows and to walk into the light of God's love.

I caution you: Do not run from the presence of the almighty, instead run *toward* the grace and the mercy of his compassion, for there is help before him. And also I caution you: Do not run from the people of God, instead run toward your forever-family who loves you and stands with you in the devastation of this moment of death. Remember, when you run to the Lord and when you run to his people you find daily grace for this dark journey. You find support to carry the weighty and hateful burden of grief that you now own.

Clearly, you will never get over this loss, but you will get through it. The sun will never shine as brightly as it did before, but it will shine. And some day the strangest thing will happen. Some day you will notice a clearing of the skies. It will come gradually, subtly, but some day you will detect within yourself the clear light of day, and with this observation you will also discover, to your surprise, that all along you owned a peace that passed human understanding, a peace that carried you and a peace only found within the arms of the Lord who never once allowed his care for you to falter, and who never once left you alone or much less the loved one for whom we mourn today.

www.ingramcontent.com/pod-product-compliance
Lightning Source LLC
Chambersburg PA
CBHW071756040426
42446CB00012B/2578